Bible Boot Camp:

Essentials

of the

Faith

volume 1

C. Michael Patton
Tim Kimberley

Credo House

ISBN: 1453856757
EAN-13: 9781453856758

Printed in the United States of America.

Credo
House

MINISTRIES

www.credohouse.org

Contents

1

TRINITY

 orientation

What to Expect?

1.   Trinity

2.   Bible

3.   Christ

4.   Man

Sections

Basic Training   Combat Training   Field Manual   Field Ops

basic training: trinity

Pine Cone

Trinity

Confession of the Trinity

We believe in _one_ God who is _One in essence_
yet _Three in Person_. All three members of the
Trinity are _eternally_ God, all of whom are
equal.

3 Primary Aspects of the Trinity

1. Only 1 God

2. Father, Jesus and Spirit are God

3. Father, Jesus and Spirit are not each other

3

Churches that believe in the Trinity:

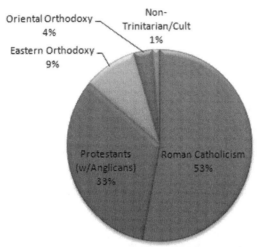

Major Christian Traditions Chart
Reclaiming the Mind Ministries 2009

Is the doctrine of the Trinity a Contradiction?

combat training: trinity

Subordinationalism

The belief that all three members of the Trinity are God, but that one or more are greater than the others.

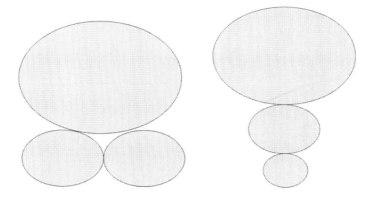

What's wrong with this view?

Tritheism
The belief that all three members of the Trinity are God, but that they are separate Gods, sharing in a similar nature.

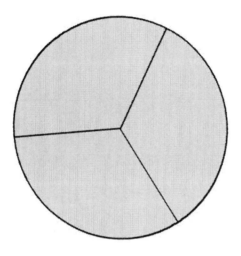

What's wrong with this view?

Modalism
The belief that all three members of the Trinity are representative of one God who shows himself in three ways.

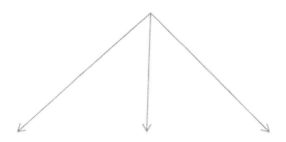

What's wrong with this view?

Nicene Creed

We believe in one God, the Father, the Almighty [pantokratora], creator of all that is seen and unseen. We believe in one Lord, Jesus Christ, the only Son of God, eternally begotten [pro panton ton aionon] of the Father, God from God, Light from Light, true God from true God, begotten, not made, of the same essence [homoousion] with the Father. Through him all things were made. For us and for our salvation he came down from heaven: by the power of the Holy Spirit he became incarnate from the Virgin Mary, and was made man. For our sake he was crucified under Pontius Pilate; he suffered death and was buried. On the third day he rose again in accordance with the Scriptures; he ascended into heaven and is seated at the right hand of the Father.

Through him all things were made. For us and for our salvation he came down from heaven: by the power of the Holy Spirit he became incarnate from the Virgin Mary, and was made man. For our sake he was crucified under Pontius Pilate; he suffered death and was buried. On the third day he rose again in accordance with the Scriptures; he ascended into heaven and is seated at the right hand of the Father.

52。

Enemies/Allies

Arius
AD 250 – 336
Believed that Christ was a created god who was like or similar to (homoiousia) the Father. Modern adherents: Jehovah's Witnesses
Condemned at the Council of Nicea in 325

Athanasius
c. 293 – 373
Believed that Christ was eternal and homoousia (of the same substance) as the Father

Sabellius
AD 215
Believed in one God who showed himself in three ways. Modern adherents: Oneness Pentecostals
Condemned at the Council of Antioch in 286

Cappadocian Fathers
(Basil the Great, Gregory of Nyssa, Gregory Nazianzus) 4th century
Helped formulate our current articulation of the Trinity

field manual: trinity

Deut. 6:4

Hear, O Israel: The Lord our God is one Lord.

Isaiah 44:6

Thus says the Lord, the King of Israel and his Redeemer, the Lord of hosts: "I am the first and I am the last, and there is no God besides Me."

John 1:1

In the beginning was the Word, and the Word was with God, and the Word was God.

2 Peter 1:1

To those who have received a faith of the same kind as ours, by the righteousness of our God and Savior, Jesus Christ.

Colossians 1:15-17a

He is the image of the invisible God, the firstborn of all creation. For by Him all things were created, both in the heavens and on earth, visible and invisible, whether thrones or dominions or rulers or authorities all things have been created through Him and for Him. He is before all things, and in Him all things hold together.

2 Cor. 3:17–18

Now the Lord is the Spirit, and where the Spirit of the Lord is, there is liberty. But we all, with unveiled face, beholding as in a mirror the glory of the Lord, are being transformed into the same image from glory to glory, just as from the Lord, the Spirit.

Acts 5:3–4

> But Peter said, "Ananias, why has Satan filled your heart to lie to the Holy Spirit and to keep back some of the price of the land? While it remained unsold, did it not remain your own? And after it was sold, was it not under your control? Why is it that you have conceived this deed in your heart? You have not lied to men but to God."

Matthew 3:16-17

> As soon as Jesus was baptized, he went up out of the water. At that moment heaven was opened, and he saw the Spirit of God descending like a dove and lighting on him. And a voice from heaven said, "This is my Son, whom I love; with him I am well pleased."

Matthew 28:19

> Go therefore and make disciples of all the nations, baptizing them in the name of the Father and the Son and the Holy Spirit.

Ephesians 2:18

> For through him we both have access to the Father by one Spirit.

What's wrong with these illustrations?

- 3-in-1 Shampoo

- 3-leaf clover

- Egg

- Water

- One person is: Husband, Son and Father

Historically Accepted illustration of the Trinity:

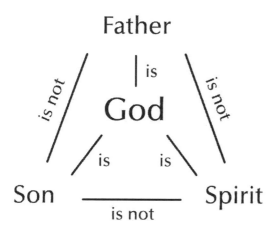

Session #1 Discussion Questions:

- How would you explain your view of the Trinity before this lesson? (were you leaning toward: subordinationalism, modalism, tritheism, etc…)

- Has your view of the Trinity changed or grown? Please explain…

- Why do you think God wants you to have a correct view of Himself?

2

JESUS

basic training: jesus

God:

All powerful
All knowing
Holy
Eternal
Perfect
unchangeable
Transendant
   Above & beyond
      all

Immaterial–
   Spirit

Love
not contrained
by Time & Space

Man:

Mortal
Material Flesh
Sinful
limited
   Get sick
walk
fail
tire

15

Apples & Oranges

Hypostatic Union

In the ~~incarnation~~ the second person of the Trinity became _fully_ _man_ while remaining _fully_ _God_. Therefore, Christ was of two natures, one person.

	Unity	Diversity
Trinity	nature	persons
Jesus	person	natures

How can an infinite God become a finite man?

combat training: jesus

Apollinarianism

Definition: Christ was God who took on a human body without a human mind/soul/spirit. The divine mind took the place of what would have been the immaterial part of man. The Word became flesh only in the sense that God took on a human body. As some have termed it, Christ was "God in a bod" or "God wearing a man-suit."

What's wrong with this view?

18

Nestorianism

Definition: Christ was fully man and fully God, and these two natures were united in purpose, *not* person. Christ was two persons with two natures.

What's wrong with this view?

Eutychianism

*Definition: Christ's human nature was _____
with His divine nature, forming a _____ nature.
Christ was from two natures before the union, but
only one after the union.*

What's wrong with this view?

"What God has not assumed is not saved." —Gregory of
Nazianzus

20

Chalcedon Creed (451AD)

*Therefore, following the holy fathers, we all with one accord teach men to acknowledge one and the same Son, our Lord Jesus Christ, at once complete in Godhead and complete in manhood, truly God and truly man, consisting also of a reasonable soul and body; of one substance with the Father as regards his Godhead, and at the same time of one substance with us as regards his manhood; like us in all respects, apart from sin; as regards his Godhead, begotten of the Father before the ages, but yet as regards his manhood begotten, for us men and for our salvation, of Mary the Virgin, the God-bearer one and the same Christ, Son, Lord, Only-begotten, recognized in two natures, **without confusion, without change, without division, without separation; the distinction of natures being in no way annulled by the union, but rather the characteristics of each nature being preserved and coming together to form one person and subsistence, not as parted or separated into two persons, but one and the same Son and Only-begotten God the Word, Lord Jesus Christ;** even as the prophets from earliest times spoke of him, and our Lord Jesus Christ himself taught us, and the creed of the fathers has handed down to us.*

Christ is 100% God and 100% man

21

Enemies/Allies

Nestorius c. 386–c. 451 Thought to have taught Nestorianism, although many challenge whether he truly taught this heresy. Condemned at the Council of Chalcedon in 451	**Cyril of Alexandria** c. 376 – 444 Fought against Nestorius, believing the term "Theotokos" (Bearer of God) should be used for Mary, the mother of Jesus, rather than "Christotokos" (Bearer of Christ).
Apollinarius Died 390 Believed that Christ had a human body, but lacked a human mind. Condemned at the First Council of Constantinople and the Council of Chalcedon in 451	**Leo I (the Great)** ca. 400 – 461 Helped articulate the nature of Christ during the Christological controversies. His tome sent to the member of the council of Chalcedon served as bedrock for the Definition of Chalcedon.
Eutychian c. 380—c. 456 Believed that Christ was of two natures before the incarnation, but only one after. Condemned at the Council of Chalcedon in 451	

field manual: jesus

John 1:14
> And the Word became flesh, and dwelt among us, and we saw His glory, glory as of the only begotten from the Father, full of grace and truth.

Luke 1:34-35
> Mary said to the angel, "How can this be, since I am a virgin?" The angel answered and said to her, "The Holy Spirit will come upon you, and the power of the Most High will overshadow you; and for that reason the holy Child shall be called the Son of God."

Philippians 2:5-8
> Have this attitude in yourselves which was also in Christ Jesus, who, although He existed in the form of God, did not regard equality with God a thing to be grasped, but emptied Himself, taking the form of a bond-servant, and being made in the likeness of men. Being found in appearance as a man, He humbled Himself by becoming obedient to the point of death, even death on a cross.

Hebrews 2:17-18
> **Therefore, He had to be made like His brethren in all things, so that He might become a merciful and faithful high priest in things pertaining to God, to make propitiation for the sins of the people. For since He Himself was tempted in that which He has suffered, He is able to come to the aid of those who are tempted.**

Luke 2:52

> And Jesus kept increasing in wisdom and stature, and in favor with God and men.

Hebrews 2:14-15

> Since then the children share in flesh and blood, He Himself likewise also partook of the same, that through death He might render powerless him who had the power of death, that is, the devil; 15 and might deliver those who through fear of death were subject to slavery all their lives.

Session #2 Discussion Questions:

What struck you most about this session?

Do you think Jesus ever got sick? If so, does that have implications for your relationship with him?

If Jesus was fully God, why did Jesus say he did not know the time of his coming? (Matt. 24:36)

Has your view of Jesus grown during this session? Would you have considered your views Eutychian, Apollianarian or Nestorian before tonight?

3

BIBLE

basic training: bible

Facts about the Bible

- *The Bible is a collection of _____ (Protestant).*

- *It was written over a period of _____.*

- *There were more than forty contributors from all walks of life.*

- *It was written in three now dead languages, _____ (most of the Old Testament) _____ (small portions of the Old Testament), and _____ (New Testament)*

- *The Bible has not been added to in over 2000 years.*

- *Christians believe that the Bible is _____ _____.*

- *Christians believe that the Bible is _____ _____.*

- *Protestant Christians believe that the Bible is authoritative over that of any other authority.*

combat training: bible

We don't have the originals and the Bible has been transmitted so many times that it is impossible to know what it really said.

The "Pass Along" activity

How do we know that the Bible we have today is an accurate representation of the original?

Bart Ehrman's Books

Many times there were errors made by the scribes who copied both the Old and the New Testaments. There are more than _____ _____ _____, called _____, in the New Testament alone.

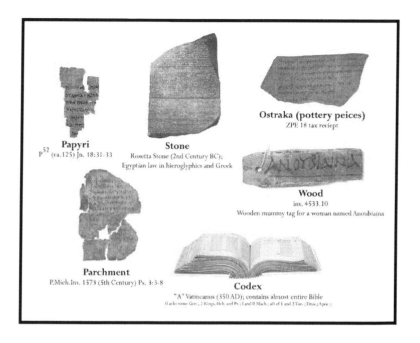

Ostraka (pottery peices)
ZPE 18 tax reciept

Papyri
P⁵² (ca.125) Jn. 18:31-33

Stone
Rosetta Stone (2nd Century BC);
Egyptian law in hieroglyphics and Greek

Wood
inv. 4533.10
Wooden mummy tag for a woman named Anoubiaina

Parchment
P.Mich.Inv. 1573 (5th Century) Ps. 3:3-8

Codex
"A" Vatincanus (350 AD); contains almost entire Bible
(Lacks some Gen., 2 Kings, Heb. and Ps.; I and II Mach.; all of 1 and 2 Tim.;Titus.; Apoc.)

Textual Criticism:
Science of reconstructing the original text of the Scriptures based upon the available manuscript evidence.

Three types of Evidence:
1. Manuscript Evidence

    a. Dead Sea Scrolls (2nd Century BC)

    b. John Ryland Papyri (125 AD)

    c. Codex Sinaiticus (350 AD)

    d. Codex Vaticanus (350 AD)

2. Early Church Fathers

   a. Codes of religion.

   b. Commentaries, diaries, books, and letters

   c. Polycarp, Clement of Rome, Justin Martyr, Ignatius, Irenaeus, Tertillian, etc.

   d. John Burgeon, a biblical scholar, catalogued over 86,000 quotations before A.D. 325.

   e. Reconstruction of the New Testament could be accomplished within 100 years of its completion using these manuscripts.

3. Translations

   a. 15,000 Copies

   b. Syriac, Old and New Latin, Sahidic, Bohairic, Middle Egyptian, Armenian, Gothic, Georgian, Ethiopic, and Nubian versions.

Author of Work	When Written	Earliest Copy	Time Span	No. of Copies
Caesar (Gallic Wars)	100–44 B.C.	900 A.D.	1,000 yrs.	10
Livy (History of Rome)	59 B.C.–17 A.D.	N/A	N/A	20
Plato (Tetralogies)	400 B.C.	900 A.D.	1,300 yrs.	7
Pliny the Younger (History)	61–113 A.D.	850 A.D.	750 yrs.	7
Thucydides (History)	460–400 B.C.	900 A.D.	1,300 yrs.	8
Herodotus (History)	480–425 B.C.	900 A.D.	1,300 yrs.	8
Sophocius (History)	469–406 B.C.	100 A.D.	600 yrs.	193
Aristotle	384–322 B.C.	1,100 A.D.	1,400 yrs.	193
Homer (Iliad)	900 B.C.	400 A.D.	1, 500 yrs.	643
New Testament	50–90 A.D.	125 A.D.	25 yrs.	>25,000

Ninety-nine percent of the variants make no theological difference. Of the one percent that do, none affect any major doctrine.

field manual: bible

2 Timothy 3:16

> **All Scripture is breathed out by God and profitable for teaching, for reproof, for correction, and for training in righteousness, that the man of God may be competent, equipped for every good work.**

Psalm 1:1-2

> Blessed is the man who walks not in the counsel of the wicked, nor stands in the way of sinners, nor sits in the seat of scoffers; but his delight is in the law of the Lord, and on his law he meditates day and night.

Revelation 22:18-19

> **I warn everyone who hears the words of the prophecy of this book: if anyone adds to them, God will add to him the plagues described in this book, 19 and if anyone takes away from the words of the book of this prophecy, God will take away his share in the tree of life and in the holy city, which are described in this book.**

2 Peter 3:15-16

> And count the patience of our Lord as salvation, just as our beloved brother Paul also wrote to you according to the wisdom given him, as he does in all his letters when he speaks in them of these matters. There are some things in them that are hard to understand, which the ignorant and unstable twist to their own destruction, as they do the other Scriptures.

1 Timothy 5:18
> For the Scripture says, You shall not muzzle an ox when it treads out the grain, and, The laborer deserves his wages.

field ops: bible

Session #3 Discussion Questions:

How could the following sentence be incorrectly copied?

"Paul went to the mall to buy apples. Paul also went to the mall to buy orangutans."

Come up with at least 3 ways this sentence could be messed up.

How does the manuscript evidence of the Bible give testimony to the uniqueness and accuracy of Scripture?

Do you want to know more about the Bible? What's stopping you from regularly growing in the Bible?

Pray that we'd all grow closer to God through a continual diet of His word.

MANKIND

Psalm 8:4
>	What is man that you take thought of him, and the son of man that You care for him?

Life Jacket

The Greatness of Man

Imago Dei: (Lat. "image of God"). Refers to the fact that humanity carries a _____ resemblance to God.

> *There are no ordinary people, it is immortals whom we joke with, work with, marry, snub, and exploit.*
> *– C.S. Lewis*

> *If individuals live only seventy years, then a state, or a nation, or a civilization, which may last for a thousand years, is more important than an individual. But if Christianity is true, then the individual is not only more important but incomparably more important, for he is everlasting and the life of a state or a civilization, compared with his, is only a moment. – C.S. Lewis*

The Fall of Man

Is man a sinner because he sins or does he sin because he is a sinner?

Original Sin

Imputed Sin

Inherited Sin

Personal Sin

combat training: mankind

Pelagianism

Definition: Man is inherently _____. The Fall did not bring condemnation upon any but Adam. Man is born like Adam with the same ability to choose between good and evil. Man sins as a result of _____ _____ that began with Adam. Grace is available *if necessary.*

Questions:

Is man morally good? _____

What is our relation to Adam? _____

Then why does man do bad? _____

Does man need the cross and grace? _____

Semi-Pelagianism

Definition: Man was affected by the fall, but not to the degree that he cannot make moves _____ _____ _____ toward God and _____ _____ _____ in the salvation process.

Questions:

Is man morally good? _____

What is our relation to Adam? _____

Then why does man do bad? _____

Does man need the cross and grace? _____

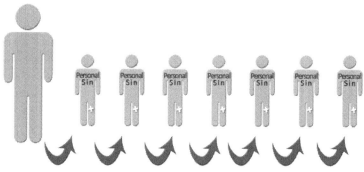

Inherited Corruption: Psalm 51:5

Augustinianism

Definition: The Fall brought _____ *and* _____ upon all men. Man is totally corrupted and inclined toward evil. Man has free will, but that will is governed by his sinful nature. Man sins, therefore, because he is a sinner.

Questions:

Is man morally good? _____

What is our relation to Adam? _____

Then why does man do bad? _____

Does man need the cross and grace? _____

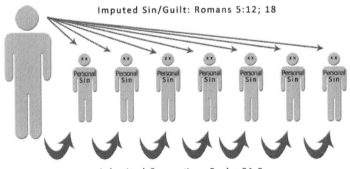

Imputed Sin/Guilt: Romans 5:12; 18

Inherited Corruption: Psalm 51:5

"Command whatever you want, but give whatever you command." - Augustine

Enemies/Allies

Pelagius	Augustine
ca. AD 354 – ca. AD 420/440 Believed that man was born without sin, having no relation to Adam. Grace was only available if needed. Condemned at the Second Council of Orange in 529	354 – 430 Believed that man was born condemned in Adam with no ability to make a move toward God outside of God's grace.

field manual: mankind

Psalm 8:4

> What is man that you take thought of him, and the son of man that You care for him?

Genesis 1:27

> **So God created man in his own image, in the image of God he created him; male and female he created them.**

James 3:8-9

> **But no one can tame the tongue; it is a restless evil and full of deadly poison. With it we bless our Lord and Father, and with it we curse men, who have been made in the likeness of God.**

Genesis 2:17

> **But from the tree of the knowledge of good and evil you shall not eat, for in the day that you eat from it you will surely die.**

Ephesians 2:1-3

> **And you were dead in your trespasses and sins, in which you formerly walked according to the course of this world, according to the prince of the power of the air, of the spirit that is now working in the sons of disobedience. Among them we too all formerly lived in the lusts of our flesh, indulging the desires of the flesh and of the mind, and were by nature children of wrath, even as the rest.**

John 3:3

Jesus answered and said to him, 'Truly, truly, I say to you, unless one is born again he cannot see the kingdom of God.'

Psalm 51:5
> Behold, I was brought forth in iniquity, and in sin did my mother conceive me.

Romans 5:19
> For as through the one man's disobedience the many were made sinners, even so through the obedience of the One the many will be made righteous.

Romans 3:10-12
> There is no one righteous, not even one; there is no one who understands, no one who seeks God. All have turned away, they have together become worthless; there is no one who does good, not even one.

field ops: mankind

Session #4 Discussion Questions:

How should the reality that man, believer and unbeliever alike, carries the *imago dei* affect the way we treat one another?

If man is truly dead with no ability to come to God on our own, how does that affect your view of salvation?

Has your view of people changed over the past session?

Credo
House

MINISTRIES

www.credohouse.org

Made in the USA
Charleston, SC
10 December 2010